CABINS, CRUMMIES & HACKS

A PAGEANT OF THE LITTLE RED CABOOSE BEHIND THE TRAIN .

VOLUME ONE: NORTH & EAST

BY

JOHN HENDERSON

(TITLE PAGE) D & H local freight leaving Whitehall N.Y. bound for Rutland, Vt., April 1968. (John Henderson)

H & M PRODUCTIONS
193-07 45th AVE.
Flushing, N.Y. 11358

ISBN 0-9629037-1-X

L.C. 90-093655

Printed By
GRIT Printing Services
208 West Third Street
Williamsport, Pennsylvania 17701

(front cover) Westbound frt. at Marysville, PA in April 1968 with an N5C bringing up the markers.

(inside front cover) Westbound B & O empties at the summit of the Alleghenies on the west end of the Cumberland Div., July 1969. Both photos by the author.

Eastbound Lehigh New England freight bound for Maybrook, NY, back on its own rails at Goshen, NY. In the foreground is the Erie mainline. (Bob's Photo)

(inside back cover) Lehigh Valley caboose A95076 in pool service on the N&W at Hammond, Indiana in Feb. 1975.

(back cover) Eastbound B & O work train descending Cranberry grade on the west end of the Cumberland Div., July 1969. John Henderson

SOURCES

CAR BUILDERS ENCYCLOPEDIA

"CABOOSES" BY COCKLE

MODEL RAILROADER

RAILROAD MODEL CRAFTSMAN

NICKLE PLATE SOCIETY PUB.

B & O SOCIETY PUB.

C & O SOCIETY PUB.

GREENVILLE CAR CO . PUB.

B & M BULLETIN

FLAGS, DIAMONDS AND STATUES PUB.

OFFICIAL GUIDE OF THE RAILWAYS

PREFACE

This is the first volume of a 3 volume set on the pageant of "the little red caboose behind the train". Volume 2, which will be out soon, covers the mid-western and southern railroads, as volume 1 covered those to the North and East. Volume 3 will cover the transcontinental roads and those of the far west. Volume 3 will also cover the cabooses of Alaska, Canada and Mexico. If demand and materials warrant there may be a volume four which will act as a supplement to the first three volumes. If you have slides you would like us to include in our subsequent volumes, please contact us at H & M Productions.

Our thanks to the many photographers who took the time to shoot the back end. Many of us, myself included, devoted most of our efforts to the front end. With the passing of the caboose, we now realize the mistake. I guess we never thought it would happen.

DEDICATION

To my Uncle, Ernest Henderson, who is always there when I need him. He is a beautiful person who has enriched my life in many ways. There is no way I can thank him enough for all that he has done.

TABLE OF CONTENTS

MAINE CENTRAL....8
VERMONT RAILWAY....15
CENTRAL VERMONT....16
LAMOILLE VALLEY....16
SANFORD AND EASTERN....17
RUTLAND....17
BANGOR AND AROOSTOOK....19
GREEN MOUNTAIN....23
BOSTON AND MAINE....24
NEW YORK, NEW HAVEN AND HARTFORD....30
DELAWARE AND HUDSON....34
GREENWICH AND JOHNSONVILLE (BATTANKILL)...43
NAPIERVILLE JUNCTION....43
NEW YORK, SUSQUEHANNA AND WESTERN....44
LEHIGH AND HUDSON RIVER....46
LEHIGH AND NEW ENGLAND....48
ERIE-DELAWARE, LACKAWANNA AND WESTERN
ERIE-LACKAWANNA....50
LEHIGH VALLEY.... 55
MORRISTOWN AND ERIE....59
CORNWALL....59
STATEN ISLAND RAPID TRANSIT....60
CHESTNUT RIDGE....60
RARITAN RIVER....61
READING....62
CENTRAL RAILROAD OF NEW JERSEY....64
LONG ISLAND....68
PENNSYLVANIA....73
PENNSYLVANIA-READING SEASHORE LINES....77
NEW YORK CENTRAL....79
PEORIA AND EASTERN....83
PITTSBURGH AND LAKE ERIE....83
CHICAGO RIVER AND INDIANA....84
PITTSBURGH AND SHAWMUT....85
TORONTO HAMILTON AND BUFFALO....86
PENN CENTRAL....88
WEST VIRGINIA NORTHERN....92
NEW YORK, ONTARIO AND WESTERN....93
FONDA, JOHNSTOWN AND GLOVERSVILLE....93
NICKLE PLATE (N. Y., CHICAGO & ST. LOUIS)....94
UNION....96
MONTOUR....97
MONONGAHELA....98
PITTSBURGH, CHARTIERS AND YOUGHIOGHENY....99
GENESEE AND WYOMING....100
IRONTON....101
BESSEMER AND LAKE ERIE....102
WABASH....103
FAIRPORT, PAINSVILLE AND EASTERN....104
YOUNGSTOWN AND NORTHERN....104
WEIRTON STEEL....105
YOUNGSTOWN AND SOUTHERN....105
AKRON, BARBERTON BELT....106
AKRON, CANTON AND YOUNGSTOWN....107
LAKE ERIE, FRANKLIN AND CLARION....107
CAMBRIA AND INDIANA....108
ANN ARBOR....109
DETROIT, TOLEDO AND IRONTON....110
LOUISVILLE, NEW ALBANY AND CORYDON....111
GRAND TRUNK-GRAND TRUNK WESTERN....112
CHICAGO AND EASTERN ILLINOIS....114
CHICAGO AND ILLINOIS MIDLAND....116
CHICAGO SHORT LINE....117
INDIANA HARBOR BELT....118
PEORIA AND PEKIN UNION....119
ILLINOIS TERMINAL....120
CHICAGO, SOUTH SHORE AND SOUTH BEND....121
BALTIMORE AND OHIO....122
BRIDLEVILLE PUBLIC LIBRARY....127
WESTERN MARYLAND....128

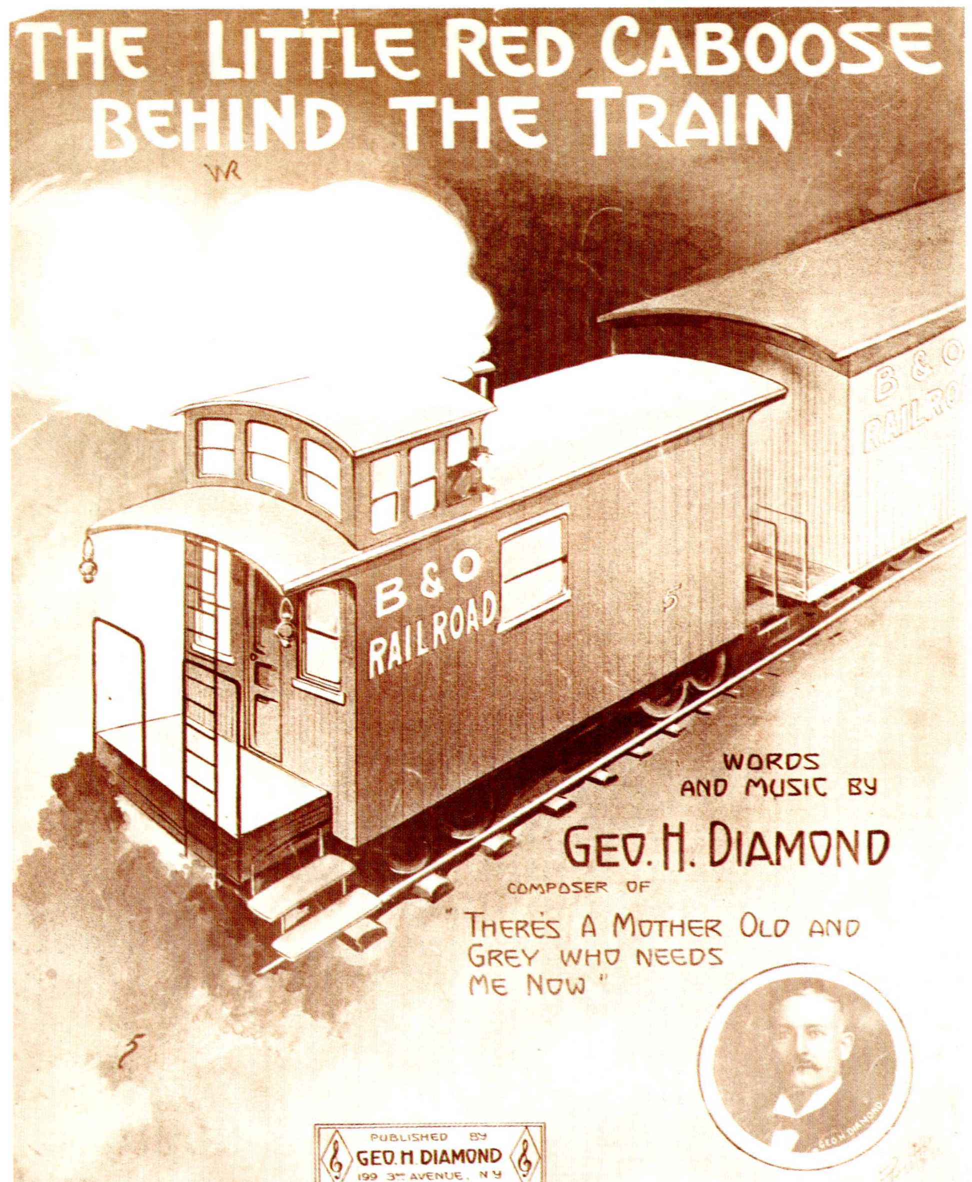

LYRICS

WHILE RIDING ON THE B&O FROM PHIL-LIE TO NEW YORK
AND MEDITATING AS THE TRAIN ROLLED BY,
SOME HAPPY THOUGHTS CAME BACK TO ME I'LL MENTION THEM TO YOU:
THE THOUGHTS OF WHEN I WAS A RAILROAD BOY;
AND IF YOU WILL BUT LISTEN I WILL TELL YOU OF THE FUN
THAT WE HAD IN SUNSHINE, SNOW OR RAIN;
WE ALL WOULD GET TOGETHER 'ROUND THE COZY LITTLE FIRE
IN THE LITTLE RED CABOOSE BEHIND THE TRAIN.

I WAS A FLAG-MAN ON THE TRAIN AND DID MY DUTY WELL,
AND ALWAYS KEPT THE SIGNALS IN GOOD TRIM,
ESPECIALLY THE RED LIGHTS THEY WERE ALWAYS IN THEIR PLACE:
ALL POLISHED UP AND BRIGHTENED WAS THE TIN;
WE ALSO USED TO COOK OUR MEALS AND EAT A-BOARD THE TRAIN.
WHEN OUR FRIENDS WOULD JOIN US WE'D RAISE CAIN;
WE ALWAYS HAD A PLENTY AND WE KEPT IT NEAT AND CLEAN
IN THE LITTLE RED CABOOSE BEHIND THE TRAIN

THE BOYS ALL NEW WHEN PAY-DAY CAME, THEY'RE WATCHING FOR THE CAR,
AND WHEN THEY SAW IT COMING UP THE GRADE,
THEY WAITED FOR THEIR WAGES, THEN THEY WOULD ALL GO UP-TOWN
BUT THE FIRST THING THEY WOULD SEE, THEIR BOARD WAS PAID
THEN WHAT A TIME THE BOYS ALL HAD A DRINKING LEMONADE
THEY SPEND THEIR MONEY FREELY MORE TO GAIN.
BUT WHEN THEY'D GET A SMALL-SIZED BUN, YOU'D SEE THEM STEERING OFF
FOR THAT LITTLE RED CABOOSE BEHIND THE TRAIN.

CHORUS

AND AT NIGHT WE'D LAY DOWN TO SLEEP UPON OUR HUMBLE COTS,
WE WOULD ALWAYS SING SOME OLD FAMILIAR STRAIN;
AND THE ANGELS THEY'D WATCH OVER US AS WE LAY FAST ASLEEP
IN THE LITTLE RED CABOOSE BEHIND THE TRAIN.

CABINS, CRUMMIES & HACKS

The little red caboose behind the train is something that we always took for granted. The fact that they are rapidly disappearing is to be expected. Technology marches on and the commonplace soon becomes obsolete. Interlocking towers, steam locomotives, semaphore signals, pullman cars, open end observations, water towers etc. either have gone, or are also in the process of being replaced. In the forty years since 1950 railroading has changed far more than in the previous forty years. Change is necessary in today's business world; intense competition makes it mandatory. While the intellect understands all this, the heart still fills with remorse as those things that made life and hobby secure and interesting are being phased out and more spartan, utilitarian and sterile replacements come on board.

The caboose has been around since the infancy of railroading. At first they were modified house cars, then flats with fitted cabins. Around the Civil War, as legend goes, a conductor by the name of T.P. Watson, who worked for the C & NW, came up with the idea of putting a hole in the roof in order to provide a better view of the train. More probably to keep an eye on his brakemen who, prior to the air brake, were running up and down the roof tops tightening, or releasing the brakes on whistle signals from the engineer.

In the post Civil War era cabooses were constructed from scratch. They started off as all wood, then went to steel over wood and then to all steel construction. As the exterior became sturdier the accommodations inside the caboose became more plush. The facilities inside early cabooses included, a coal stove for heat and as a place to cook meals, a desk or work space for the conductor to work over his waybills and bunks for making the hack a home away from home for crews that worked on branches without a hotel or YMCA. The car also was a convenient place to store the tools used to make running repairs on the train. The caboose also had a primitive lavatory facility. Basically, it was a rolling outhouse that at least gave the crewman some privacy. Water was usually carried in a 5 gallon milk can and sinks were of a rudimentary nature.

Later on all these facilities were brought up to date, flush toilets, axle or engine powered generators that provided electric light and refrigeration. Oil heat replaced the coal stove and a permanent watertank was added, making caboose travel a much more comfortable experience.

Radio communication between locomotive and caboose , or between trains and either the dispatcher or the tower, made things safer and eliminated much of the necessity of leaving the caboose to hand signal the engineer, or to use a line side phone.

Cabins, crummies and hacks are just a small sample of the jargon railroad men have used to describe their home away from home. Other terms of endearment used on the caboose are buggies, waycars, shacks, doghouse, jailhouse, hash hut and a whole assortment of other monikers that sound terrible, but belie a certain affection.

MAINE CENTRAL

The Maine Central connects all the population centers of Maine, along with a branch serving northern New Hampshire.

When it came to the purchase of non revenue equipment, such as cabooses, the Maine Central management was trying to either make the Guiness Book of Records for longevity, or they were just plain thrifty. By the way, when scanning these MEC photos the rule is; follow the bouncing tree. The way it moves around you get a sensation similar to that of using a nickelodeon.

On the MEC, World War one era wood cabooses led long productive lives. In appearance, 582 is closest to as built. 587 kept its original truss rods, but was given new side panels and outside bracing on the cupola. 559, 603 and 606 have had new roofs, cupolas and side panels added and some have had their truss rods removed. Additional modifications have been made to the bodies of 610, 616 and 635.

Frank Szachacz

Frank Szachacz

Frank Szachacz

Frank Szachacz

Frank Szachacz

Frank Szachacz

Frank Szachacz

Frank Szachacz

Frank Szachacz

Frank Szachacz

Frank Szachacz

647, 648 and 649 were built on the chassis of old express reefers, retaining their original length and riveted passenger trucks. (leaf taken from the same book used by the Bangor and Aroostook)

The MEC's first foray into the steel caboose era was done on the cheap, by buying old, circa 1937, excess stock from the Western Maryland. 660, 662 and 663 are examples of these ex-Western Maryland hacks, with one of the four side windows blanked out after purchase. Except for the added end windows, they were similar in construction to a design found on the Lehigh Valley, Reading and Jersey Central.

658 and 659 were purchased direct from the manufacturers. This was the MEC's first real opening of the purse strings in a half century. Flushed with success MEC made a second plunge in the mid seventies and purchased extra wide vision models like the 643 and 653. This was the last caboose purchase made before absorption into the Guilford system.

Portland Terminal RR, which is a subsidiary of the MEC, had even tighter wallets. They modified boxcars, such as the PTM 1, into transfer hacks.

Frank Szachacz

R. Wallin Coll.

Frank Szachacz

Frank Szachacz

Joe Quinn

Frank Szachacz

Frank Szachacz

John Benson

(this page) A modern steel caboose #656 trails a freight out of Nothern Maine Junction.

(next page) #670 a member of the team of hacks that made up Maine Central's last purchase of cabooses. Here she is found clearing Rigby yard, Maine in Sept. 1982. Frank Szachacz

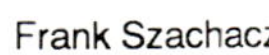

Frank Szachacz

MAINE CENTRAL
THINK SAFETY
670
WORK SAFELY

VERMONT RAILWAY

The Vermont Railway arose like a phoenix bird from the ashes of the Rutland in 1963 through the grace of the State of Vermont. The Rutland had been consumed in a labor management conflagration. The State wanted to see that the communities stretched along the 125 miles from Burlington to Bennington Vt. were not deprived of railroad service.

#2 and #6 are wood sided with a steel underframe. Their most distinguishing difference is the cupola window configuration. The Central Vermont, Grand Trunk and New York Central railroads had hacks of a similar design.

#8 is a bay window type purchased from the Bessemer and Lake Erie.

A. Mitchell

Bill Folson

Henry Maywald

CENTRAL VERMONT

The C.V. is a Canadian National subdivision running from Brattleboro, Vermont to New London, Connecticut, a distance of 121 miles.

The influence of C.N. extends to its cabooses. 4012 was built in 1912 and is identical to those 3 window wood hacks found on the rest of the C.N. and Grand Trunk.

John Benson

LAMOILLE VALLEY

Formally the St. Johnsbury and Lamoille Country RR, the Lamoille Valley continues to serve the 96 mile route from St. Johnsbury to Swanton Vermont with trackage rights into St. Albans.

#200 is an ex-New Haven NE5 caboose wearing the reverse colors of the Rutland.

Bob's Photo

Norton Clark

SANFORD AND EASTERN

The S&E is a long abandoned 31 mile Pinsley shortline that ran from Cumberland Mills to Sanford, Maine.

#11 is an ex-Boston and Maine hack, that has a uniquely designed, very narrow cupola with a record setting 12 windows. All this, along with another ten windows on the sides, makes this the most "paneful" caboose on any railroad; presenting a view more appropriate to the bridge on a ship. I guess folks in Maine are true down-easters.

A. Mitchell

RUTLAND

The Rutland was a 392 mile RR that reached from southerly, White Creek and Bellows Falls, Vermont; via Rutland, to northerly, Rouses Point N.Y. A Branch also reached westward across upper New York State from Rouses Point to Ogdensburg. It was abandoned after a lengthy strike that started in 1961.

An end cupola, four window, wood caboose of New York Central vintage, #12 comes in red with white lettering. It derives from a series numbered 10 thru 49.

#28 is similar to #12, but contains only three windows a side.

Except for the later two tone paint scheme, #42 is identical to #28.

#50 is an extended vision caboose built to D&H specifications. It too, carries the new image paint scheme.

Bob's Photo

Bob's Photo

BANGOR & AROOSTOOK

M. D. Winkley

The BAR is a 557 mile line serving the northern and eastern parts of Maine. Filled with yankee ingenuity, down east railroaders have come up with an interesting collection of one-off hacks. A few traditional crummies, however can be found on the property. C-70 sports the classic design of the NE type caboose. It has wood sheath construction, a cupola and three to four windows a side. Maine is a state with long cold winters and a thin population, making for remote branches and primitive living accommodations. Cabooses had to be able to provide greater comfort than those on roads operating in more moderate climes. Necessity being the mother of invention, and furthermore, the financial inability to purchase more sumptuous hacks from the manufacturers, resulted in the BAR taking steam locomotive tender chassis that were no longer needed

John Benson

Frank Szachacz

and building on them larger than normal cabooses. These were more like rolling hotels which could be a home away from home for crews that might be on the road for days. This is especially true if a blizzard, which is a common occurrence in the North East, blew into town. C-44 is an example of this type of construction. The side door is a feature that was found only on a few railroads, like the Frisco and the Illinois Central. They were handy for passing things from one train to another, or for loading supplies from a high level freight platform. Some railroads blanked them in, feeling that they were a safety hazard. Single track railroads, like the BAR, felt that there was little danger of a crewman falling out the side door into an oncoming train.

Frank Szachacz

Ben Perry

C-65 is much longer, indicating that a freight car chassis was used in its construction. C-67 from the same series has a different window placement, otherwise their features are similar to C-44. In earlier years, C-67 appeared in grey paint with red, white and blue trim. Later on some of them were modernized by having their cupolas removed and a bay window affixed to the side, in addition the side doors were removed from C-68 and C-69.

With the end of WW2 surplus military equipment, such as Pullman Standard troop sleepers, were available at bargain rates. Yankee traders, like the management of the BAR, jumped on these bargains and purchased some for modification into cabooses. They retained their allied trucks and side doors, but bay windows, possum belly tool boxes and radios were added. Some of the sleeping accommodations were removed to provide space for the other necessities of caboose life.

C-86, C-91 and C-94 illustrate the many variations this type of caboose comes in . C-99 proudly displays the later paint scheme and the novelty of an extended porch on the end. C-10 in a blue scheme, carries an unusually large bay window. It was possibly used for inspection purposes, because a large number of people could take advantage of its special viewing angle.

Bob's Photo

Frank Szachacz

Frank Szachacz

Frank Szachacz

Frank Szachacz

GREEN MOUNTAIN

The Green Mt. was founded by Nelson Blount of Steamtown fame. It operates a former Rutland branch that runs for 52 miles from Rutland to Bellows Falls, Vermont.

#51 is an off center, bay window caboose that came over from the Bessemer and Lake Erie and is painted in the green and yellow livery that was common to Rutland's hacks.

John Benson

Frank Szachacz

Frank Szachacz

BOSTON & MAINE

The B&M operates north from Boston to Portland, Maine and West from Boston to Rotterdam Jct. N.Y. Branches emanate all over, covering parts of the states of Massachusetts, New Hampshire and Vermont.

On the B&M, railroad men refer in slang to cabooses as "buggies" and on this road there are many variations of the buggy. Early steel buggies have red ends reminiscent of the wooden caboose era.

C25 was built in the mid 30's and is of a design similar to the Pennsy N5 cabin car. Over th years it has sported two different size heralds and has had screens applied to the windows.

C11 and C34 display two variations of the lettering and of the color blue. Originally numbered 104700-104723, they had their numbers reduced to C11-C34.

C1-C10 and C40-C49 are NE5 type buggies. C4 and C9 were originally red in appearance, they were repainted McGinnis colors in the 60's and then monotone blue in the 70's.

Frank Szachacz

Frank Szachacz

Frank Szachacz

C127 is an updated version of a steel buggy, but it retains the trucks of the 10400 series.

C52, along with renumbered 452, 262, 466, 470, 480 and 482 are all 24 foot steel, center cupola, two side window buggies. They illustrate the many differences that exist in window placement and lettering schemes.

C161 in McGinnis colors and C496 in all blue are examples of transfer buggies.

C496 has red ends that have darkened with age.

A 104000 series buggy in the original all red with traditional logo leaves Wells River, Vermont with a milk train in 1954.

104003 a buggy from the same class, is also an NERS wide monitor, long hack with boxcar red sides and caboose red ends.

104647, on the rear end of a freight, is an NERS, four window, narrow monitor, all wood buggy.

Frank Szachacz

Frank Szachacz

John Benson

Frank Szachacz

Frank Szachacz

John Benson

Richard Louderback

A. Mitchell

(next page) B & M freight clearing Greenfield Jct., Mass. in June 1966.
John Henderson

A. Mitchell

A. Mitchell

TRAX
12291
ARMOUR
C 23

R. Wallin Coll.

Eric Archer

Bob's Photo

Bob's Photo

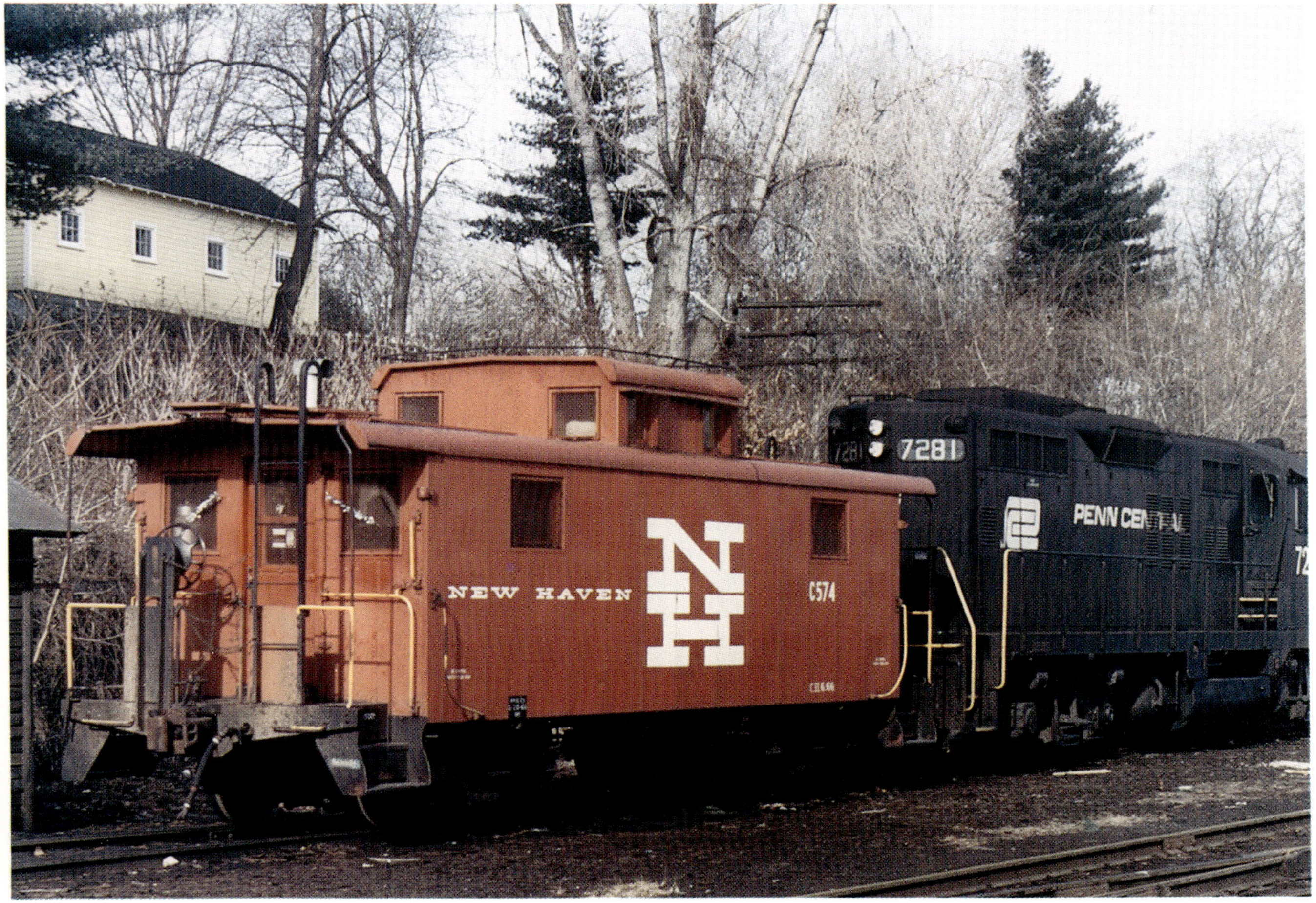

Bob's Photo

NEW YORK, NEW HAVEN AND HARTFORD

The New Haven was a large class 1, that ran from New York to Boston, via New Haven, New London and Providence. It had branches to Danbury, Waterbury, Hartford, Springfield, Maybrook, the Cape etc.

The series, designated class NE5, is numbered C510-C634. They were built in the early 1940's by Pullman Std. 616, 511, 574 and 566 are adorned with the varied paint and lettering schemes that have appeared over the years. The full name is proudly displayed on the side of 616. 511 wears the "McGinnis" colors of a black roof, with red sides and a large black and white NH. 574 wears the last scheme, all red with a white NH. The moment captured here is bittersweet; 574 is adorned with Christmas ornaments, but soon its old identity will be obliterated by the Penn Central, whose locomotive is pulling it along. 566 gets no respect, it's shorn of its name, and it has been demoted to wreck train service.

Classed NE6, C635-C709 were built in the late 1940's by International Car and Equipment Co. The NE6s are one foot longer than the NE5s and were the last series the New Haven bought before the merger. 681 wears the classic black, with red and white lettering, while 708 wears "McGinnis" colors. 664 wears the latest simplified livery of plain red with white lettering.

Bob's Photo

Frank Szachacz

(left) C623, a class NE5 cabooce, runs shoemaker style on a local freight led by New Haven diesel switcher 0993 in a Christmas card scene. Bob's Photo

(right) C674, a class NE6, leaves Southampton St. yard, Boston in August of 1963. Bob's Photo

NEW HAVEN
C-874

(left) Triple caboose hop of non-reinforced, wood hacks pulled by an ALCO RS-3 arrives in Whitehall, N.Y. in April 1968. John Henderson

(next page) 35703, a steel reinforced hack, on the end of a southbound freight north of Mechanicsburg, N.Y. in April 1968. John Henderson

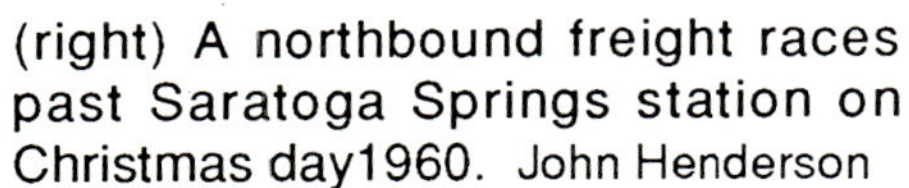

(right) A northbound freight races past Saratoga Springs station on Christmas day1960. John Henderson

RADIO
CAYUGA ROCKSALT CO. INC.
DELAWARE & HUDSON
35703
RADIO

John Benson

DELAWARE & HUDSON

The D&H is a bridge road that connects Canada with major trunk lines in New York and Pennsylvania.

The 35700 series wood, road cabooses have steel reinforced frames and ends. A development brought on by the use of articulated steam locomotives as pushers out of Binghampton, N.Y. and Scranton, PA. They destroyed regular wooden hacks; therefore, until the arrival of all steel cabooses the 35700 series were the backbone of the fleet. 35700 had its cupola removed. 35703R has a restriction on her underframe that demotes her to online use only. 35704, 706 and 707 illustrate the different lettering styles and colors used on this series. The first ten hacks of the 35700 series were constructed in 1942 from boxcars that were built in 1907 by ACF.

Richard Louderbach

The 35800 series are all wood with non-reinforced ends. Available for use all over the system their more fragile construction limited them mostly, in the days of steam, to service north of Albany. 35819, 845R, 872 and 921 promenade the various liveries found on this series of hacks.

35852 and 35932 are wooden crummies with their cupolas positioned towards one end, rather than the traditional center. Note the extra tall windows on 35852, they extend almost to the roof line. 35932 has been fitted with outside bracing and 35940 displays the later herald. 35922 has had its cupola removed and appears to be on the way to cremation.

When they bought the first all steel bay window cabooses, like 35721, they were delivered in yellow, probably to draw attention to them as something new and different. When they were outshopped however, they went back to traditional red, as on 35726 and 35813. 35804 and 35729 with extended porches appear to be home built variations of the bay window type. 35084 later appeared in two tone grey and maroon.

DELAWARE & HUDSON
35932
RADIO

DELAWARE & HUDSON
hold
RADIO

HUD
DELAWARE AND HUDSON
35940

DELAWARE
&
HUDSON
35721
RADIO
THE BRIDGE LINE
TO NEW ENGLAND
AND CANADA

When Conrail was formed in the late 70's the D&H became the beneficiary of its locomotives and rolling stock. 35801 came from the Lehigh Valley and 35793 came from the Reading.

35710 and 35712 and 35713 are examples of D&H's first purchase of extended vision cabooses. Just like the earlier ones there are many variations in lettering.

John Benson

D &
3580

RADIO
DELAWARE & HUDSON

John Benson

D & H
35729
LT WT 41200

RADIO
D & H
35793

Frank Klock

David Hamley

David Hamley

John Benson

GREENWICH AND JOHNSONVILLE BATTANKILL

The G&J was once known as the Battankill railroad, a D&H subsidiary that runs for 16 miles from Greenwich Jct. to Thompson N.Y.

35823 seems to be a huge number for a caboose from such a small railroad; however, it is compatible with the D&H numbering scheme. It's a four window, wood, transfer caboose, with added side bracing.

35803, lettered for the Battankill, was an old, sans cupola, D&H wood caboose.

NAPIERVILLE JUNCTION

The N.J. is the D&H's Canadian connection; taking D&H trains from Rouses Point, N.Y., the thirty odd miles, to Montreal, Canada.

#36 is an old wood, end cupola, two side window hack kept together by extra outside bracing and sway cables on the undercarriage.

David Hamley

NEW YORK, SUSQUEHANNA AND WESTERN

Before becoming a major regional carrier, the "Suzie Q" was a 63 mile short line. It originated at the Hudson River and meandered across northern New Jersey to a connection with the Lehigh and Hudson River at Sparta Jct.

There were 9 cabooses on the property, numbered 0110-0119. 0110 is red with yellow lettering. The way its windows are boarded up, it appears the railroad had a policy of not replacing broken windows.

0116 is red with white lettering. Beside having its full complement of windows, metal awnings have peen placed over the side windows.

117 on the end of an eastbound freight at Little Ferry, N.J. John Henderson

Allen Roberts

N Y S & W
0117
Ship and Travel
SANTA FE
—all the way
ATSF
19969
Santa
SP
SOUTHERN
PACIFIC

You don't have to in an International

EXTRA WIDE VISION CABOOSE

Today's trend toward higher, wider freight cars gives a trainman two alternatives. He can stick his neck out — or — ride comfortably and safely in an International Extra Wide Vision Caboose.

Railroads with vision are going this route.

If you seek greater efficiency from your crews plus greater economy of operation, look into International Cabooses. If you don't see what you want, we'll build them to your specifications.

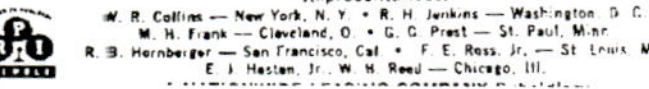

LEHIGH AND HUDSON RIVER

The L&HR is a connecting line that joins with the New Haven and Erie RR's at Maybrook, N.Y. and with the Lehigh Valley and Jersey Central at Easton, PA.

Cabooses on this railroad tell the story of the long and the short. The longs, such as #18, are standard NE types. The shorts are four wheel bobber cabooses. #81 shown here, was the last four wheel hack still in active service. She saw use on the local freights that ran to the zinc mines.

Charles Hauser

Westbound Lehigh and Hudson River freight departing Maybrook N.Y. in May 1965. Bob's Photo

John Henderson

LEHIGH AND NEW ENGLAND

The L&NE has been abandoned since Oct. 31, 1961. Originally it had a total of 177 miles of track; starting in the North at Cambell Hall, N.Y., it ran southwest across northern New Jersey to Martins Creek, Allentown and Hauto, Pa.

567 departs Martins Creek on that fateful day with the last coal train. It was built by Magor in 1924 and was extra long with a steel underframe necessitating two stoves, one on each end to keep the large interior warm. Crewmen still complained that it was too cool in winter.

512, appearing in its pre-1961 lettering, was one of the four, 4 wheel bobbers to survive until the end of operations. Made of wood with a steel underframe, it was built by American Car and Foundry in 1918.

577, on a caboose hop, was of composite construction which Magor built in 1930.

580 and 581 are all steel hacks built by the Reading for the L&NE from their NMk plans, the only difference from those found on the Reading are the trucks. A total of 5, numbered 580-584, were built. 581 has a simplified logo, a cost cutting move brought on by mountains of red ink.

Bob's Photo

Bob's Photo

John Gwinn Coll.

Marty Zak

ERIE-DELAWARE, LACAWANNA & WESTERN ERIE-LACKAWANNA

The EL was a major, class 1, East-West railroad stretching from New York City on the east coast to Chicago, Illinois in the mid-west. Buffalo N.Y. is a major branch terminal.

4967 is a traditional Erie, 3 window, wood, center cupola hack with one cupola side window.

The 800 series cabooses, such as 880, 897, 900 and 906, were purchased by the DL&W in the 50's to replace an aging fleet of wooden cabooses, like #701. They were the first to be radio equipped. The radios were battery powered, with axle generators to recharge the batteries. They were also the first to have electric marker lights. 897 is dressed in the fashion of pre-merger Lackawanna.

Marty Zak

Karl Henkles

Karl Henkles

T33 is one of a series of transfer cabooses built in early 69 and used in yard areas all over the system. Just like the CNJ, these hacks have roof mounted reflector disks for locomotive headlights.

04942, shown here in wreck train service, was one of the last wooden hacks from the Erie on the system.

C125, 129, 150, 177, 182, 202 and 259 are standard Erie all steel cabooses; they were the backbone of the fleet until the arrival of the bay window type. C-177 is still lettered Erie.

346 and 366 are examples of the bay window cabooses that replaced them.

C324 is an ex-Erie bay window, dressed up in EL's last pre-Conrail paint scheme.

Allen Roberts

Frank Szachacz

Robert Warren

Bob's Photo

Karl Henkles

Karl Henkles

LEHIGH VALLEY
LV
95 020

Jim Sorensen

LEHIGH VALLEY

The "Route of the Black Diamond" was an 1,100 mile railroad whose mainline streached from the Hudson River to Buffalo, NY. Along its route the L.V. served the coal producing region of northeast Pennsylvania.

The L.V. numbered its cabooses in the 95001-95500 series and all of these hacks were of the standard northeast NE type.

95048 is in traditional L.V. attire. This hack has the unusual feature of porthole windows on the ends. A feature that was possibly influenced by the L.V's association with the Pennsy.

When passenger service flourished on the road, "Route of the Black Diamond" was proudly emblazoned on the sides of these cabooses .

After the demise of the passenger service, 95064 had a safety slogan affixed to its side.

When hacks, like 95053, were outshopped during the sixties, the safety slogans were dropped and the LV inside a black diamond began to appear.

Because the railroad traversed rough neighborhoods at each end of the line 95023 had movable, screen shutters mounted on its side windows.

The "A" in front of 95093 and 95067 denotes that these hacks were available for pool service. 95067 was blessed with two chimney pipes. Something must have been really cooking in this crummy.

(preceeding page) Lehigh Valley hack 95020 departs Allentown, PA. in Sept. 1972 behind a depress center flat. Bob Wilt

William Brennan Coll.

Walter Matuch

Frank Szachacz

Robert Wilt

Allen Roberts

95016 has been freshly outshopped. The absence of the "A" means she must stay close to home and unlike her previously mentioned sisters with the "A" all her shutters are movable.

Various color combinations have been tried over the years. 95054, 1776 and 95015 promenade some of those combinations. 95054, like Phoebe Snow, came dressed in white. Notice the black diamond now comes as an embelishment on a flag, very prophetic since the L.V. was soon to be a fallen flag. 1776 displays the L.V's feelings about our 200th anniversary. 95015 acts as a bellwether for L.V's upcoming merger with Penn Central by trying out P.C. green.

Walter Matuch

John Henderson

MORRISTOWN & ERIE

The M & E is a ten mile shortline in Northern New Jersey operating between Essex Fells and Morristown.

This caboose has a rather dimunitive cupola window and is wood sided with a steel underframe. It appears to be of Erie lineage.

CORNWALL

A 12 mile shortline, the Cornwall runs from Lebanon to Mount Hope Pa.

This is an ex-Reading NM type caboose that is unmodified, except for paint and lettering.

John Gwinn Coll.

Allen Roberts

STATEN ISLAND RAPID TRANSIT

The S.I.R.T. is a B&O subsidiary operating a twenty six mile railroad on Staten Island, with a branch to Cranford Jct. New Jersey. Primarily a rapid transit line, it does maintain a local freight service.

Ironically, the B&O was not the supplier of hacks to the S.I.R.T. #4 is an ex-Reading NM type caboose.

CHESTNUT RIDGE

Originally 11 miles long and now 7, the Chestnut Ridge ran from Palmerton to Kunkletown in eastern Pennsylvania.

#602 has had its cupola removed, making it a very long transfer hack.

Jim Sorensen

RARITAN RIVER

The Raritan River is a freight only shortline operating in New Jersey.
The hacks used on the line came from several railroads and all are done up in an attractive paint scheme. #6 came from the Lackawana, #7 is an ex New York Central and #10 is an ex New Haven that was built by Pullman Standard.

READING

Bob's Photo

The Reading had a 1,268 mile network of small lines that covered south eastern Pennsylvania, including the four main cities, Philadelphia, Reading and Harrisburg and Trenton, N.J.

Reading, NM class, all steel cabooses have been made since 1924. They have welded underframes and Duryea cushioned gear and Taylor trucks. Cabooses of a similar vintage were built for the CNJ, Lehigh Valley and Western Maryland railroads. These cabooses started out with eight side windows and as they were periodically out shopped various windows blanked out. When they were repainted from an all red with white lettering paint scheme to a yellow top and green bottom with green lettering scheme the window frames were changed to aluminum. The side windows had separate top and bottom panes and sliding type windows were used on the cupola sides. 94044 of class NMo and 92887 of class NMI are shown as built. In this format they survived into 1966, but the future can be seen on the cabooses lurking in the background. Another view of a class NMI caboose shows 94018, built in 1944, sporting the traditional red paint and lettering. It also had a new method of mounting the air lines, using fixed pipes rather than flexible hose on the undercarriage. Later on, like 92898, it sported a monochromatic green body paint with yellow lettering.

Even cabooses in the same series can have variations. 92917 and 92926 were built in 1941 and classed NMI. Because of different interior modifications they were sporting different patterns of blanked out windows when photographed in the early seventies. 94064 of class NMp, built in 1948, shows a variation of a different sort, a lower side vent was used, rather than the more traditional roof vent.

John Gwinn Coll.

William Brennan Coll.

Prior to the Reading being absorbed into ConRail a purchase was made of wide vision, all steel, cabooses. They came with the latest technological features, roller bearing trucks, cushioned underframe and radio. The photo of 94101, class NEa, was taken in Hagerstown Maryland two months after its manufacture in August 1970 .

CENTRAL RAILROAD OF NEW JERSEY

The Jersey Central, now part of Conrail, operated a 192 mile line that streched from Jersey City, N.J. to Scranton, Pa. It also had a network of small branches.

At the end, the series 91155 thru 91394 were the oldest cabooses on the CNJ. Originally they had wood sheathing, but in an economic rebuilding, plywood siding had been applied, however, all of them had steel underframes.

The four examples above illustrate the many variations that have come about over the years. 91369 had its cupola removed and was used in yard and transfer service. 91309 had its cupola windows blanked out when it was downgraded from road service. 91158 and 91351 illustrate different stages of paint condition and repair.

91500 series, class NE, all steel cabooses were similar to Readings NMI class, but operated on Andrews trucks. Other visual difference are the blanking out of the stove window and the placing of awnings on the cupola windows. They differed from the earlier wood cabooses in the following ways: they came with seven side windows, four on one side and three on the other, with no end windows. End windows were present on the wood sided cabooses and then dropped with the conversion to an all steel body. The lack of a fourth window on one side was due to the placement of the stove, it had been moved from the corner location it had enjoyed in the wood ones. An intriguing feature is the missing second railing at the top of the ladder on the ends. The orange circle on the cupola ends provided a reflective surface for locomotive headlights. No, it was not there to improve the aim of wayward youths.

Matthew Herson

91507, photographed in East Allentown in June of 1971, carries the original paint scheme of this series.

91509 shows the condition, before refurbishment, that this cash poor railroad let their cabooses get into . 91539 and 91534 sport a more eye catching paint scheme. The lettering is red on white, rather than white on red and on each side the striping is slanted in opposite directions. When the striping was simplified to its present form, as on 91501 and 91552, the direction of the slant was made the same. With the advent of stripes the appliances were painted white, instead of the traditional yellow.

R. Wallin Coll.

Norman Kohl

LONG ISLAND

The "Route of the Dashing Commuter" is the largest passenger operation in America; however, it has a large local freight service that covers all of the islands communities. At one time an independent, the L.I. was absorbed by the Pennsylvania railroad and today it is operated under the auspices of the State of New York.

#16, an N52A wood type caboose with a steel underframe, was manufactured by A.C.F. in the early twenties.

#27 and #50, are examples of the old and the new teamed up together. #27 is similar to #16, while #50 of class N22, is an all steel hack built in 1958 by the International Car Co.

C56 and C61 are of the N22A class, they were also built by the International Car Co. in 1961. C56 comes to us attired in both L.I. and M.T.A. colors. C61 has a slightly different window arrangement.

C63 is the first of seven class N22B hacks built by Int. Car Co. in 1963. C63 displays both L.I. and M.T.A. color schemes.

C62 is similar to the N22Bs, but has smaller side windows and no ribbing on the roof.

#1 is one of two ex-Pennsy N5 cabooses, whose cupola windows have been blanked out and its been demoted to yard service.

C91 is an ex-Illinois Central side door hack purchased by the L.I. in 1972. The side door was subsequently blanked out.

C72 was purchased from the defunct New York, Ontario and Western. It's wood sided and the small side window is for the lavatory.

C24 is wood hack of the N52A class. It's similar to #16, but is painted in the Long Island's more contemporary pre- M.T.A. colors.

Eric Archer

Eric Archer

Frank Szachacz

Norman Kohl

Norman Kohl

Westbound freight with caboose C-56 passing tower "B" in Bethpage , Long Island during Feb. 1979. It's coming off the Central branch from Ronkonkoma. The connecting track from the Southern division is in the foreground. Henry Maywald

(next page) Lengthy for the Long Island, C-62 and C-69 accompany an eastbound Port Jefferson branch freight at Huntington in Nov. 1963. Norman Kohl

C-69
C-69
LONG ISLAND
C-62
LONG ISLAND
B&O

PENNSYLVANIA
478043
8533
PENNSYLVANIA

Bob's Photo

Marty Zak

PENNSYLVANIA

"The Standard Railroad of the World" was America's largest railroad. Its lines blanketed the middle Atlantic states and the original North West Territory.

True to its legend, the standard railroad designed and built its own cabooses, much the same way it designed and built its own steam locomotives. Being different, "P" Company men refer to their home away from home as a cabin.

980815 and 980020 are N6Bs, built during the World War One era, mainly for lines West. 980815 has the original paint scheme of tuscan red sides with a black, steel underframe. 980020, which serves the Philadelphia region, has a larger logo and a spelled out name, also the cupola is painted black.

477174 and 477301 are N5s. 477174, built in 1917, has orange sides; while 477301, built in 1926, has a red body with a black cupola. 477174 appears to have been side swiped while serving the Philadelphia region. Her injuries have not prevented her from bravely carrying on.

476998, 477632 and 477701 were built at the beginning of World War Two. Classed N5B, 477632 wears the early scheme, with a spelled out name and specified for service on the Pittsburgh region. 477701 is painted orange with a simplified herald; in addition, the cupola proudly proclaims that she is radio equipped. 476998 has a grey cupola which designates her for north-south pool service. GG-1 4839 is moving this caboose hop through Journal Square, Newark on the way to Harsimus Cove.

(previous page) A caboose hop with class N8, 478043 pulled by switcher 8533 on the Delaware River bridge between Trenton, N.J. and Morrisville PA. in July 1963. John Henderson

John Gwinn Coll.

Marty Zak

Allen Roberts

Marty Zak

477879, 477990 and 477982 are N5Cs, which were built at the beginning of WW2. The Lionel Corporation built a beautiful scale model of this cabin and blamed it on a whole host of railroads. The yellow cupolas on 477879 and 477990 indicate they were available for east-west pool service. 477990 carries the Pennsy's distinctive radio antennas on its roof. 477982 bears the earlier more traditional lettering.

478104 comes from the last major cabin design built by the Pennsylvania Railroad. Designated N8, it's assigned to the Eastern Region and totes an unofficial, unsolicited political comment.

#237 and #250 operate on the Pennsylvania, Reading Seashore Lines in New Jersey. #237 is an ex-Pennsy N5B with a P.R.S.L. herald. #250 is an ex-New York Central transfer hack lettered for the P.R.S.L. It arrived via the Penn Central merger.

Marty Zak

Frank Szachacz

Karl Henkles

(upper right) Pennsy ALCO switcher 9102 drills Cove yard in Jersey City with a homemade, yellow tansfer caboose in April 1962. Matthew Herson

(right) 477814 an N5B, which operates in east-west pool service, rounds the "shoe" eastbound in Dec. 1968. R. Wallin Coll.

NEW YORK
CENTRAL
SYSTEM
TRAILER TRAIN
TTX 903665

Allen Roberts

John Henderson

NEW YORK CENTRAL

The "Water Level Route" is a super class 1 blanketing all of the northeast. Anchored as it was in the East by New York City and Boston; it reaches, via Buffalo, Chicago and St. Louis in the West, serving just about every city, town and hamlet in-between. The New York Central System had many subsidiaries, principal among them were the Michigan Central, Boston and Albany, The Big Four and the Pittsburgh and Lake Erie.

19654 is representative of the 19000 series. They were 35 foot long and had wood sides and a steel underframe and were built in the early 1900's by the Merchants dispatch Transit, a N.Y.C. subsidiary.

17042, part of the 17000 series, is three foot shorter than the 19654 and has a different cupola window arrangement. It operated on the Boston and Albany and was similar to hacks found on the Central Vermont. Cabooses of this series were built during the World War one era.

2705 is a cupolaless hack operating on express reefer trucks. It's used on mail and express trains that carry no passengers.

20093 is a wood sided, center cupola caboose that, if it were steel sheathed, would resemble the NE type caboose that was common on the Reading and the Lehigh Valley.

18008 was built in 1966 and is 32 foot long.

(preceeding page) Eastbound New York Central Freight brings new 1968 Chevys to market while passing through South Schenectady, N.Y. on its way to Selkirk yard. John Henderson

R. Wallin Coll.

Bob's Photo

Matthew Herson

Matthew Herson

Bob's Photo

John Gwinn Coll.

20368,20391, 21787 and 20500 are steel bay window cabooses built in the late forties and early fifties. 20368 comes from the N7A class, 20298-20497, and was built in 1952 by St. Louis Car Co. 20931 has similar lineage, but has had three additional slogans embellished on its sides: (1) "Road to The Future, (2) Safety and Service and (3) Prevent Loss and Damage". 21787 is decked out in the modern jade green paint with the cigar band herald. When it was rebuilt in the early sixties the stove was converted from coal to oil and a full electrical system was installed. (Note the multiplicity of stacks on the roof.) 20500 is ex-B&A, built in 1949 at the DSI shops in East Rochester. Like 20391, it too had slogans a'plenty on the sides: (1) "Keep alert to safety first, (2) Safety and service and (3) Road to the future". It also bragged of being radio equipped.

21496 was assigned to the NYC subsidiary, Peoria and Eastern. Before rebuilding, 21787 was identical in appearance to 21496.

R. Wallin Coll.

John Benson

John Benson

David Hamley

Karl Henkles

David Hamley

502 and 518 are from the P&LE, they look at first glance to be identical; however, closer inspection reveals that 502 is made of rivetted construction, while 518 is welded.

530 is an ex-Union Pacific class CA-9.

531 is an International caboose that is not of parent New York Central design.

#20, which hails from the NYC subsidiary the Chicago River and Indiana railroad, is a box car cum transfer hack.

John Benson

PITTSBURGH & SHAWMUT

The P&S operate in a north-easterly direction from Freeport Jct. near Pittsburgh, to Broadway, 88 miles away.

#194 is a freshly repainted Pullman Standard caboose that's similar in style to those built for the New Haven. 194 appears here with and without the company herald.

191 is an ex-Erie-Lacawanna caboose.

196 & 197 are ex-Lehigh Valley hacks. 196 has the bicentennial motif.

150 is a boxcar cum caboose, the dreadnought end belie the change.

David Hamley

David Hamley

David Hamley

David Hamley

David Hamley

John Benson

John Benson

TORONTO, HAMILTON & BUFFALO

The TH&B is a 111 mile line that connects Buffalo, N.Y. with the towns and cities of Ontario, Canada, notably Toronto. Since 1987 it has merged its operations with the Canadian Pacific.

#62 is a bay window hack with storm windows. It has two stoves and is obviously setup to provide comfort throughout long, severe winters.

It also uses extended vision type cabooses, such as #83, that are manufactured from Canadian Pacific specifications.

TH&B #80 follows an identical Canadian Pacific caboose on a C.P. freight.

Frank Szachacz

PENN CENTRAL

The Penn Central is the result of a 1968 merger of the New York Central, Pennsylvania and New York, New Haven and Hartford railroads. It's identity survived until 1976, 8 years later, when it was absorbed into Conrail.

Penn Central's caboose fleet is composed of cabins left over from its respective pre-merger railroads. Until the arrival of Conrail blue, jade green, a New York Central color, was the standard shade of the caboose fleet .

19064 and 19269 are ex-Pennsy class N5's, built in 1917. 19269 was assigned to the N.Y. region.

22990 R is an ex-Pennsy N5B restricted to local use.

23010, 23045 and 23136 are ex-Pennsy N5Cs. 23045 serves the Canada region.

William Brennan Coll.

David Hamley

William Brennan Coll.

R. E. Minnis

William Brennan Coll.

23321 is an ex-Pennsy class N8.

18422 is an NE type that comes from the Lehigh Valley. It's designated for service on the eastern region.

19825 is an ex-New Haven class NE6.

23633 of class N8A and 23512 of class N8B are ex-New Haven hacks that were rebuilt in 1970, with the addition of a bay window on the side and the blanking out of the cupola.

21757 a class N7A and 21031 a class N7B are ex-New York Central. 21499 is from the Peoria and Eastern, which is a subsidiary of the New York Central and now Penn Central.

18261 is a ex-NYC class N9 transfer hack, built in 1968.

18529 is an ex-NYC class N11E.

John Gwinn Coll.

John Gwinn Coll.

William Phillips

WEST VIRGINIA NORTHERN

An eleven mile long branch line that serves the coal mines, the West Virginia Northern connects with the Baltimore and Ohio at Tunnelton, W. Virginia.

The gaudy paint job fails to hide the B&O parentage of this old, wood sided NE type caboose.

William Brennan Co'l.

Charles Hauser

NEW YORK, ONTARIO & WESTERN

The NYO&W operated a 545 mile railroad from the Hudson River, near New York City, to Oswego on Lake Erie, with branches into the coal fields of north eastern Pennsylvania. In 1957 it was largest railroad to ever go belly up.

#8343 is a wood sided hack operating on express reefer trucks. There are three windows on one side and two on the other.

FONDA, JOHNSTOWN & GLOVERSVILLE

The "Sole Leather Line" connected with the New York Central at Fonda, NY and served the leather tanning industry of Johnstown and Gloversville. The FJ&G was absorbed by the Delaware and Otsego.

#3 is an ex-Delaware and Hudson caboose.

Norman Kohl

NICKLE PLATE

Bob's Photo

The New York, Chicago and St.Louis operated a parallel competing line to the New York Central from Buffalo west to Cleveland, Detroit, Chicago and St. Louis. The Nickle Plate was absorbed by the Norfolk and Western in 1964.

There are three basic series of hacks on this road: the venerable wood 1000s, the ex-Wheeling steel, standard cupola 700s and the modern bay window 400s.

1115 was built in 1901 at the Nickle Plate's Stony Island shops. Here she is bringing up the markers on a westbound freight at Farmdale, Illinois in 1958. The 1000's originally had wood frames but were converted to steel in the 1920s. They were built over a 44 year span from 1881 to 1924. After the N&W merger, they were all phased out, with the last being destroyed in 1972.

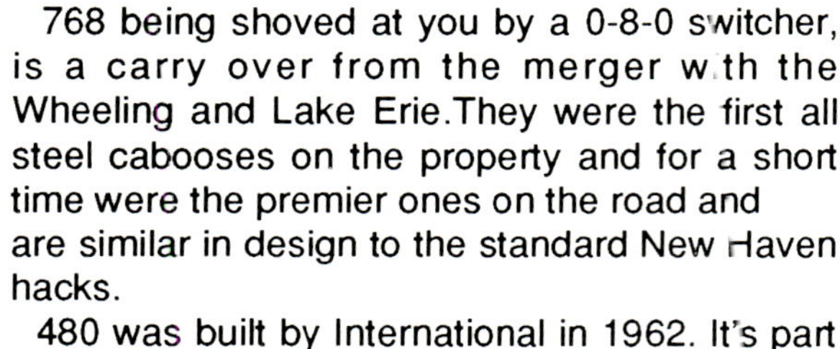

768 being shoved at you by a 0-8-0 switcher, is a carry over from the merger with the Wheeling and Lake Erie.They were the first all steel cabooses on the property and for a short time were the premier ones on the road and are similar in design to the standard New Haven hacks.

480 was built by International in 1962. It's part of the last built group in this series and International's redesigning has erased some of its Nickle Plate lineage. The most noticeable exterior difference between these cabooses and the earlier 400s is the lowering of the bay window. The high speed service lettering had also undergone modifications over the years and they were radio equipped some time after construction. Used all over the system, most have survived into the present serving the N&W.

Karl Henkles

R. Wallin Coll.

John Benson

David Hamley

John Benson

David Hamley

UNION

The Union RR is a 38 mile transfer line located in the Pittsburgh area. It's not to be confused with the Union RR of Oregon.

All of its hacks are second hand. Some came from the Erie, but C-104, a long bay window, is an ex-B&LE and #1030 is a short bay window.

120 is an odd homebuild with picture windows and a scalloped fringe on the rear of the roof. The lattice work end rails are reminiscent of the French Quarter in New Orleans. All we need are vines and magnolia's to complete the picture.

C21 is a 24ft. hack built by Greenville with Durea underframe, its cupola has been removed.

C1002 is a 30 ton hack modified by the railroad with the addition of a bay window.

C1023 is a similar caboose with the exception of the bicentennial paint scheme.

David Hamley

David Hamley

David Hamley

MONTOUR

A 45 mile line connecting Montour Jct. to Mifflin Jct. Pa.

#36 & #38 are ex-Union Pacific class CA-9 cabooses with commonwealth trucks in two different color schemes.

David Hamley

David Hamley

David Hamley

MONOGAHELA

A ten mile shortline that gained brief notoriety when it operated ex-N.Y. Baldwin sharks.

#153 is an old truss roded wire car from the Pennsy that the Monongahela uses as a maintenance caboose.

#72 a Pullman Standard caboose that has had tool boxes added to the chassis.

David Hamley

David Hamley

PITTSBURGH, CHARTIERS AND YOUGHIOGHENY

a seven mile shortline running from McKees Rocks to Carnegie, PA.
97 is an ex Union Pacific class CA-5 caboose.
99 is a second hand International hack.

Charles Hauser

GENESEE & WYOMING

The G&W is a twelve mile long short line located in eastern Pennsylvania. (The use of Wyoming in the name refers to a local valley not the state.) Its primary function is to bring salt to market.

Over the years the G&W has purchased second hand hacks. #8 is an ex-Lacawanna wood caboose. As the wood cabooses wore out they were replaced by steel cabooses, like #11, which came from the Western Maryland. The windows were replaced and W.M. red was exchanged for orange.

#10 is another second hand rebuild. oil heat has been added, notice the oil filler nozzle high up on the side, also many of the side windows have been blanked out.

John Benson

Bob's Photo

IRONTON

Jointly owned by the Lehigh Valley and the Reading, the Ironton is a very short, 8 mile railroad that operates between Hokendauqua and Ironton, its main purpose is to haul sand and gravel.

#4 is a four wheel bobber type.

#6 is an ex-Reading NE type with boarded up windows on the cupola and one boarded up window on the side.

#7 is a wood, end cupola hack with three side windows.

Bob's Photo

Bob's photo

John Benson

David Hamley

BESSEMER AND LAKE ERIE

The B&LE runs in a north-south direction across western Pennsylvania. Its main purpose is to bring iron ore from boats on Lake Erie to steel mills in the Pittsburgh area.

1955 is a road class NE1 bay window caboose that was built in 1950 by the Greenville Steel Car Co. of Greenville, Pa. The interior is fully equipped with bunks, lockers, stove and refrigerator.

1999 has a centered bay window, unlike 1955 which has it placed towards one end, a metal awning protects the window on the side. All the other windows have been blanked out.

#1981 is an International caboose done up in bicentennial livery. The interior appears more plush than the regular caboose. The rear compartment looks like a furnished office. Notice the large vents on the side. suspect air conditioning.

David Hamley

WABASH

The Wabash with over 2,300 miles of track ran from Detroit and Toledo westward to Chicago, St. Louis, Kansas City Omaha and Des Moines.

02233 used in transfer service carries the follow the flag symbol.

2740 is a standard, steel over the road caboose that somehow escaped the cupola streamlining of the late forties.

2602 is a wood version of the steel caboose and has an inoperable cupola because of its demotion to transfer service.

Karl Henkles

Karl Henkles

Karl Henkles

FAIRPORT, PAINESVILLE & EASTERN

The F,P&E serves as a terminal switching line for Fairport Harbor and Perry, Ohio.

#200 is a plain wood sided transfer hack painted yellow with black lettering.

YOUNGSTOWN & NORTHERN

John Gwinn Coll.

The Y&N is a five mile long switching line that serves the mills, furnaces and industries of Youngstown, Girard and McDonald, Ohio.

#47 is one of five transfer hacks on the property. It's steel sided and painted yellow with black lettering.

WEIRTON STEEL

Weirton Steel operates an industrial shortline in Weirton, West Virginia.

#3, named Montreal, is decked out in bicentennial attire and appears to be air conditioned. It's all steel and has an unusual cupola window pattern. The ends appear to be reinforced and the handrails on the sides of the ends turn inward in a unique fashion.

David Hamley

David Hamley

YOUNGSTOWN AND SOUTHERN

A 35 mile line running south from Youngstown to Darlington, Ohio. #31 is an ex-Union Pacific class CA-5 caboose.

AKRON, BARBERTON BELT RAILWAY

The A&BBR is a 23 mile long switching line running between Akron and Barberton, Ohio.

The caboose used on this line came from the military, via the Lehigh Valley RR. It was purchased in the Mid 60's and was painted red with yellow lettering. Later on it was painted in a shade of gold with a black roof and black diagonal stripes on the end, along with the removal of one side window.

John Benson

John Gwinn Coll.

John Gwinn Coll.

LAKE ERIE, FRANKLIN & CLARION

The LEF&C is a 15 mile shortline connecting Clarion to Summerville, PA. It had interchanges with the Penn. and the Central.

#11 is an ex-Lehigh Valley, NE type caboose with port hole end windows and screens over all the other windows.

AKRON, CANTON & YOUNGSTOWN

The ACY runs for 121 miles across northern Ohio.

65 and 67 are built quite differently.

65 has three windows, while 67 has four, 67 is all red, while 65 has yellow ends.

John Benson

CAMBRIA & INDIANA

The C&I is a 30 mile long short line in western Pennsylvania.
Small but proud, the C&I wears its patriotism on its caboose.
#56 is a 30 foot long, steel, center cupola hack wearing two different paint schemes.
#53 is an ex-Pennsy cabin classed N5B.

John Benson

David Hamley

David Hamley

ANN ARBOR

The Ann Arbor RR, once independent, became part of the Wabash system and eventually the Detroit, Toledo and Ironton. After the DT&I was mergerd in 1984with the Grand Trunk Western the Ann Arbor was taken over by the State of Michigan.

The Ann Arbor runs in a north westerly direction from Toledo, Ohio. It crosses the lower Michigan peninsula to Boat Landing on the shore of Lake Michigan. There it connects with three car ferry routes the Ann Arbor operated on Lake Michigan .

2701 is a transfer hack in traditional dress.

2823 is a 3 window hack with an off center coupola.

2837 is an ex-Wabash in the latest state owned paint scheme.

Henry Juday

R. Wallin Coll.

David Hamley

DETROIT, TOLEDO AND IRONTON

The D,T&I originally ran from Detroit to Ironton a distance of 365 miles. Merged several times; since 1984 the D,T&I has been part of the Grand Trunk Western.

#102 is an early steel caboose with the later herald.

#125 is a contribution from a previous merger with the Wabash and Ann Arbor. It carries a safety slogan and a very sharp logo.

#134 is a standard NE type built by International with two side and no end, windows. Beautifully attired in red with a yellow cupola and one of my favorite lettering jobs.

#143, also from International, has an off-center cupola with the early herald.

999550 is not technically a caboose, it's a bunkhouse car for work train service. It does however, have mounting brackets for rear end markers.

David Hamley

David Hamley

R.E. Minnis

David Hamley

Bob's Photo

David Hamley

David Hamley

GRAND TRUNK & GRAND TRUNK WESTERN

During the last century Canadian National chose not to label its U.S. possessions with the word Canadian. Therefore, Grand Trunk was coined as a name for its New England operations and Grand Trunk Western for those in Michigan. Both Grand Trunks have a combined mileage of 1,152.

GT75952 and 75955 are three side window, end cupola cabooses. Its traditional styling can be found on many railroads, but the cupola, however is of a design unique to the C.N. and its subsidiaries. 75952 sports the traditional herald while 75955 carries the modern abbreviated logo, along with a switch from brown to red paint.

GT75960 is a steel, extended vision hack with a large picture window on the side. It's probably there to catch as much sun as possible in the cold northern latitudes.

GT-DT&I 153 is a modified International hack that has a new heating system, resulting in the blanking out of some windows.

GTW75011 is similar to 75955, except for the steel sheaths mounted over its original wood sides, giving it a Santa Fe style appearance.

GTW75176 is an example of a DT&I caboose that has been re-lettered and renumbered to conform to the Grand Trunk. Even the DT&I's bicentennial caboose wasn't spared.

#114 is a center cupola, steel covered hack that has been repainted and remarked, but not renumbered.

Eric Archer

John Benson

LOUISVILLE, NEW ALBANY & CORYDON

An eight mile shortline connecting Corydon Jct. to Corydon, Indiana. #1883 is a wood caboose with a modified bay window.

John Benson

David Hamley

Mike McIlwaine

John Benson

John Benson

John Gwinn Coll.

CHICAGO AND EASTERN ILLINOIS

The C&EI is shaped like a tree with Chicago as the northern base and with three branches in the South ending in St. Louis and Chaffee, Missouri and Evansville, Illinois. In 1976 the C&EI was "buzz sawed" into the Mo. Pac. system.

The C&EI has a diversified group of road and transfer cabooses. All of their grab irons and handrails are uniquely adorned with black and white safety stripes.

#1 was built by the Magor Car Corp. of New Jersey, a home to many a similar C&O caboose.

#16's cupola is reminiscent of the Wabash, but it is homemade, a bit oversized and one of several on the property.

#36 is a steel bay window hack. C&EI's cabooses display the symbol of modernism "radio equipped," a slogan that has adorned the crummies of several railroads, starting with the Erie.

#438 is a traditional three window, wood caboose with a tall, outside braced cupola. C&EI hacks are unique for having both their complete name and initials boldly spelled out on the side.

#512 is a transfer hack painted in a brighter red than the almost brown that adorns most road cabooses. It was bought brand new in the mid sixties from the International Car Corp. of Buffalo, N.Y. Most of the other cabooses seem to be either second hands, or home rebuilds.

#517 is a transfer hack that was built on a flat car chassis. It's black undercarriage differs from the norm, usually the cabin and chassis are painted the same color.

John Gwinn Coll.

Karl Henkles

Karl Henkles

John Gwinn Coll.

CHICAGO AND ILLINOIS MIDLAND

The C&IM operates a 121 mile line from Peoria to Taylorville, Illinois. It functions primarily as a coal hauler.

The standard type cabooses are numbered from 34 to 70. 42, 63 and 68 display the various paint combinations in use. They are rebuilds, completed around 1941 and no expense was spared to provide the utmost in comfort for the crew. Full kitchen facilities were provided, including a stove, refrigerator, sink and cupboard. Three berths, oil heat and electric lights round out the luxuries in these mobile homes on rails.

73 is an extended vision caboose with a simplified color scheme. Its purchase made necessary by the long coal drags.

John Gwinn Coll.

John Gwinn Coll.

John Benson

HIGH . . . WIDE and HANDS

EXTRA WIDE VISION CABOOSES

The extra sight we afford them of the train ahead, the comfortable seat provided, the many safety measures that surround them, the conveniences at every hand — all add up to the reasons why International Extra Wide Vision Cabooses have the reputation of providing trainmen passenger car comfort plus the peak of railroading reliability.

Standard or custom-built interiors — each with an opulent array of options. Write for brochure.

INTERNATIONAL CAR CORP.

835 ENGLEWOOD AVENUE • BUFFALO, N. Y. 14223

Representatives:
W. R. Collins — New York, N. Y. • R. H. Jenkins — Washington, D. C.
M. H. Frank — Cleveland, O. • G. G. Prest — St. Paul, Minn.
R. B. Hornberger — San Francisco, Cal. • F. E. Ross, Jr. — St. Louis, Mo.
E. J. Hasten, Jr., W. B. Reed — Chicago, Ill.
A NATIONWIDE LEASING COMPANY Subsidiary

John Benson

CHICAGO SHORT LINE

The CSL is a 30 mile long switching line that connected with 37 different railroads in the Chicago area.

#1 is a modified ex-Santa Fe hack whose cupola windows have been blanked out because of its demotion to transfer service.

INDIANA HARBOR BELT

Originally a subsidiary of the New York Central and Milwaukee Road, the IHB serves the Chicago switching district and northwestern Indiana. The IHB provides interchange services and maintains a huge icing facility for refrigerator cars.

#7 is a converted freight car chassis with roller bearing trucks, re-manufactured for use as a transfer hack.

#33 has Florida East Coast heritage. It runs on express reefer trucks and is liveried in the new image paint scheme.

#92MW, minus a bay window and cupola, has conventional trucks and is a transfer caboose assigned to maintenance of way service.

John Benson

John Benson

John Benson

PEORIA & PEKIN UNION

Peoria, Illinois is the meeting point for fourteen railroads. As such, it serves as a transfer point second only to Chicago and St. Louis. The P&PU's role is to act as a switching outfit for these line haul carriers.

In 1966 there were seven transfer hacks on the property. #204 appears to have been home built on a flat car chassis.

#220 was constructed in Dec.1970 on an older caboose chassis.

#230 has Santa Fe lineage and a colorized herald, along with several blanked out side windows.

Karl Henkles

Karl Henkles

John Benson

ILLINOIS TERMINAL

The I.T. is a 355 mile long, class 1 RR that connects Peoria and Champaign, Illinois with East. St. Louis, Ill. The I.T. maintains belt lines around all the principal cities on its routes

The New York Central was the mentor for I.T's hacks. 802 is a wood transfer hack with a steel bay window. The lettering and color are reminiscent of the N.Y.C.

985 and 988 are steel bay window cabooses built from N.Y.C. plans. 985 wears white, while 988 wears a combination of green and yellow. Both are equipped with oil stoves and full electrical systems.

Karl Henkles

Karl Henkles

Karl Henkles

John Benson

CHICAGO, SOUTH SHORE & SOUTH BEND

The CSS&SB connects Chicago with the steel mills in the Gary and South Bend areas. Eighty seven miles long the CSS&SB operates an electric MU commuter service along with its freight operations.

329 is an ex C&O steel hack built by Magor.

999008 This ex-Santa Fe caboose carries the largest number I've seen. It retains its Santa Fe number and the South Shore logo has been placed over the Santa Fe herald.

10001 is also of Santa Fe lineage, th e last digits of its number are repeated on the cupola and several of the side windws have been blanked out.

John Benson

John Benson

BALTIMORE & OHIO

The B&O, "which connects thirteen great states with the nation", links Baltimore and Washington D.C. with Chicago, Cincinnati, Indianapolis and St. Louis. Branch lines blanket Ohio, western Pennsylvania and New York. The B&O lost its independence when it was absorbed into the Chessie System in 1973.

As one of the largest of eastern roads, the B&O had a huge caboose fleet with 27 different classes of hacks.

400 cabooses of the I-1 class were built and this example, C-360 is of 1913 vintage. Notice that the cupola windows are boarded up, a fate that befell many of the B&O's wooden cabooses.

C-465 and C-1406 are classed as I-1A and are among 134 of these cabooses built during the early twenties from the same plans as the I-1s. C-465 had half of her windows boarded up during some internal restructuring. C-1406 has been demoted to transfer service, her cupola has been removed and she has been painted yellow.

Karl Henkles

Karl Henkles

Karl Henkles

Karl Henkles

Karl Henkles

Karl Henkles

C2054, C-2065, C-2078, C-2098, C-2165 and C-2278 are all class I-5. I-5s are similar in shape and size to the I-1s, but the ends and the bracing are made of steel, not wood. Another distinctive difference is that the cupola sides are slanted instead of straight. 400 I-5s were built during the late twenties. C-2054 is as built. C-2065 has had its side windows removed and was repainted yellow. C-2078, C-2098 and C-2165 have variations in the number of side windows. Note the early herald on the sides and the green end door common to this series of hacks. C-2278 has had its side windows shuttered and its ends painted yellow.

C-2888 and C-2896 are of the C-17A class. Both of these cabooses were built in 1956 and differ only in paint scheme. Except for the conventional roof, this class was a further development of the wagontop design. They represent the last road hacks B&O built for itself.

Bob's Photo

R. Wallin Coll.

R. Wallin Coll.

C-3715, built in 1971, is a C26 class bay window caboose. C&O had some constructed from the same plans.

90747 is a C&O class C8 wood sided caboose renumbered for the B&O and was built during the late twenties.

2701, built in 1943, is a class I-16 . This example from the 2700 series is an ex-box car.

C-1896, C-1901 and C-1902 are modified I-1s and had their cupolas removed. They were used in transfer service by the B&O subsidiary, Chicago Terminal Co.

Karl Henkles

Allan Roberts

Karl Henkles

Karl Henkles

(left) Eastbound B & O coal drag races down seventeen mile grade through Piedmont, West Virginia with export coal. John Henderson

Karl Henkles

BRIDLEVILLE PUBLIC LIBRARY

It's amazing the purposes a caboose can be put to; here it serves as an annex to a library, possibly to help keep students minds "trained" on their studies. 2160 is an ex-B & O class I-5 hack who arrived in Bridleville, Pa. through the courtesy and generosity of the local Kiwanis International club. David Hamley

R. Wallin Coll.

WESTERN MARYLAND

Western Maryland is the junior partner in today's Chessie System. Anchored in the East by Baltimore the railroad runs west, via Hagerstown, to Cumberland MD., there it forks into two routes, one route serves West Virginia and the other western Pennsylvania.

Variety is not the appropriate word to use when describing the caboose fleet of this railroad. They used a design similar to the Reading's NMj class, minus the external tool boxes. Three color schemes were employed over the years. The first, not represented here, was red with a black roof and a circular herald.

1842 and 1892 display the second paint scheme of a red body with white speed lettering and stripes. 1892 has had screens placed over the windows, a feature lacking on 1842.

1871 flaunts the third schemes circus colors of red and white sides, black roof and black speed lettering. The circus colors were first phased in during outshopping in the late 60's.